SHORT TAKES ON
THE APOCALYPSE

SHORT TAKES ON THE APOCALYPSE

PATRICIA YOUNG

BIBLIOASIS
WINDSOR, ON

FIRST EDITION

Library and Archives Canada Cataloguing in Publication

Young, Patricia, 1954–, author
        Short takes on the apocalypse / Patricia Young.

Poems.

Issued in print and electronic formats.
ISBN 978-1-77196-135-6 (paperback). ISBN 978-1-77196-136-3 (ebook)

        I. Title.

PS8597.O67S56 2016   C811'.54   C2016-902735-X

                                                                            C2016-902736-8

Edited by Anita Lahey
Copy-edited by Allana Amlin
Typeset by Ellie Hastings
Cover designed by Chris Andrechek

 Conseil des arts Canada Council
du Canada   for the Arts

 ONTARIO ARTS COUNCIL
CONSEIL DES ARTS DE L'ONTARIO
50 YEARS OF ONTARIO GOVERNMENT SUPPORT OF THE ARTS
50 ANS DE SOUTIEN DU GOUVERNEMENT DE L'ONTARIO AUX ARTS

 Canadian   Patrimoine
Heritage   canadien

Published with the generous assistance of the Canada Council for the Arts and the Ontario Arts Council. Biblioasis also acknowledges the support of the Government of Canada through the Canada Book Fund and the Government of Ontario through the Ontario Book Publishing Tax Credit.

PRINTED AND BOUND IN CANADA

 MIX
Paper from
responsible sources
FSC
www.fsc.org   FSC® C004071

CONTENTS

2. *Too Many Guns in the House*

for Terence

S<small>PUN</small> S<small>HRUNK</small> B<small>ROKEN</small>

THE KINDNESS OF HUTTERITES

*I am oppressed with a dread of living forever. That is the only
disadvantage of vegetarianism.*

–George Bernard Shaw

When the boy enters the farmers' market the Hutterite women
shake their heads and cluck their tongues. He stops at their stall
Saturday mornings to stock up on vegetables. But carrots will fatten
up no one. Chard and cucumbers won't put meat on his bones.
A heavy-set, robust people, the Hutterites can still remember the
starving centuries. Even now, in this land of plenty, their DNA
carries the memory of that old world hunger. Poor kid, they mutter,
shoulder blades sticking out like the beginning of wings. But the
Hutterite women (bless their pacifist hearts) are getting on. At three
score and ten, their eyesight has dimmed. They can't see that the
boy is much older than they are, he's older than Methuselah, son
of Enoch, grandfather of Noah. That he's outlived thirty-six wives,
fathered more than three hundred children, that his great-great-
grandchildren are like the stars. Potatoes, the women say, offering
the boy a free, ten-pound bag. This is good food. Go home. Eat.

THE FIRST VEGANS

> *Heart attacks—God's revenge for eating*
> *his little animal friends.*
> —Anonymous

In the beginning Adam and Eve spent their days gaping.
Their eyes bulged and their jaws hung slack.
Look at this. What's that? Who made that hooting sound? Did you?

They gaped at the persimmon-streaked sky,
a dewdrop balanced on the tip of a leaf.
The moon! Dangling white orb. They gaped
at water, the way it trickled over rocks
and through their fingers. Gaped at each other,
their wondrous beauty, and also their own twiddling thumbs.

They wandered the garden, plucking breakfast
off trees. Pulled lunch out of the ground.
Munched and grazed through dinner.
Like the other herbivores, their intestinal tracts
were long and convoluted, their molars flat.
Even the dirt tasted good enough eat.

In time they grew bored of Eden's cornucopia.
Life had become a succession of peeling rinds, grinding nuts,
spitting out husks. One morning Eve woke with strange
hankerings so set to work inventing things:
knife, spoon, pot, recipe. Experimented
with roasting and broiling, sauces and marinades.

You're a genius, babe, Adam said, nuzzling her neck
after a hard day of naming the animals.
Puleease, she said, it's the least a helpmeet can do.

Evening meals were now elaborate feasts,
after which they'd make buoyant love, then gape
at each other until they fell into a deep and heavenly sleep.

The first baby arrived. Then another and another.
Every nine months a baby popped out. Eve was fond of them, sure,
but they were so helpless and needed her, body and soul.
                              Soul?
She furrowed her brow. Adam, honey, what's a soul?

No time now for chopping or dicing, mashing or mincing.
Who had the patience for de-seeding a pomegranate
just to garnish a yam and chickpea tajine?
Vegetables were more demanding than babies.

And then the night in bed when she moaned:
Can't do it anymore. Hack up another cabbage.
Besides, the kids hate cabbage, hate turnip, hate eggplant.

Adam grunted. Want me to speak to Yahweh?
Eve stroked her husband's belly, her fingers like the tendrils
of young pea shoots. Oh no, she whispered, don't bother Him.
You're a smart guy. You'll think of something…

CARNIVORE BRAIN

*...the time will come when men such as I will look upon the murder
of animals as they now look upon the murder of men.*
—Leonardo da Vinci

The cutlets on your plate remind you of something,
you can't remember what, but it doesn't matter

because the bodies of animals are leaking
onto the tablecloth, they are bleeding onto your lap.

What does it matter? Remember the day you tripped
on the sidewalk, walking too fast, oblivious

of the bumps and dips in the pavement?
Your suddenly split knee weeping plasma and platelets?

The cutlets on your plate remind you of someone—
the man you had sex with later that evening

after a meal of red meat and red wine. You can't
remember his face but that doesn't matter because

this is no vegetable reverie, this is your carnivore
brain rolling that man in butter and crumbs.

Does it matter that you can't remember his face?
That the cutlets on your plate remind you of nothing?

BITE

When I walk into the house
the dog lunges. It's a beautiful animal,
intelligent, with black curls. Okay,
so the dog doesn't actually bite me,
just nips my heel. Still. A large canine
with fear or malice on its mind. I kneel
inside the hallway, nursing the teeth marks
as the dog's owner rushes forward
and clamps its jaw shut. She whispers something
I can't hear, a reprimand, a few harsh words,
but the dog is already forgiven
the way a child is forgiven,
his mother's embrace swallowing him up.

A mother's embrace will swallow up
her child. He's forgiven the way
he's forgiven. The dog was
reprimanded with a few harsh words,
its jaw clamped shut. She whispered something
(the dog's owner) as she rushed forward
while I nursed teeth marks. In the hallway
I knelt, no fear or malice on my mind.
My heel had been nipped. Still. A large canine.
The dog didn't actually bite me,
okay. Intelligent with black curls,
it was a beautiful animal, the dog that lunged
when I walked into the house.

WHO'S LOOKING AT US NOW?

Lightning is just the flash on God's camera when He's taking a selfie.
                                                              –High Taco

We're striking a pose, not tongue-cheeked or duck-mouthed, but classic, cat-style and arched. Regard our side-to-side tilt, our up-or-down. In awe of the dying world, we're striking as soloists, prune-lipped and chin-jutted. How do you like us in profile? Not criminal or combative, sensual not sonic, artful not exhibitionist, lazy and generic—that's us, more or less. In the vanguard position, we're riding seahorses, sparrow-faced and cheep-cheep. We're diving like foxes into deep snow. Masterful greeters, boom and bust posers, brazen flaunters, a triumph of nature, born now and tagged here. Stand back while we mount the Kama Sutra in smiling arrangements. Clavicle and nape-conscious, grin-tilted, startled, exactingly groomed to appear sexily dishevelled. How can you not be a little impressed?

DANZA DE LOS VIEJITOS (DANCE OF THE OLD MEN)

A man growing old becomes a child again.

–Sophocles

In the village without tears the gods never ran out of jokes.
They *were* a running joke. An in-your-face joke,
un-nuanced, a parody breaking into
a complex dance routine. Furthermore,

sleep was a joke, food was a joke, sex was a joke,
even the sun setting behind the red-tiled roofs
was a phenomenon that evoked laughter. *Our laughter.*
Imagine us laughing into a mirror and the gods laughing back.

Ah, yes, tears of mirth.

And then we were standing at the edge of a zocalo,
watching miniature gods in wool ponchos and baggy
white cotton: old men, old men pink-faced as boys.

How they coughed when they trembled.
How they tottered when they stomped.
Click-clack, ha-ha, no kidding, we found ourselves
noticing wooden shoes, corn husk masks,
a hand-written sign on a barber shop door: *Hola Michoacan.*

In the village without tears, we drank Blue Agave.
Tequila, for god's sake. Who drinks tequila?

Gringo turistas?

There's a Mexican proverb that says
time spent laughing is time spent with the gods.
And so it was for us, whiling away whole afternoons
in the presence of hook-nosed campensinos.

And so it was for them, small toothless gods who'd outlived
the Conquistadors—one minute hunched and tapping their canes—
the next   over our heads   leaping...

STORY TIME

You know how it is in the kid's book world;
it's just bunny eat bunny.

–Anonymous

At one you follow your mother's voice up the moon
ladder and down a fireman's pole. At two you can utter

vague jabberings (the beginnings of a philosopher's
musings?). Is that you, Glub-Glub, sitting on a bench

carved out of a stump, listening to your granny read
the sad tale of a lady goose who goes mad for love?

Drop that blanket over your head, make a tent
of silence. You're three now, so, yes, you may hop

down the wooded trail and knock on the door
of the tree house with the acorn lantern. Your best

friend, Squirrel, lives there. At four you understand
that bunnies sing in rock bands. Their egos are fragile.

When frightened they leap out of their cotton tails.
You're disappointed at five: fewer pictures, more words.

But the plots have sharpened. Animals with big teeth
and night vision skulk around the margins. And then

it happens, in the blink of a pink eye the alphabet cracks
the world open. On your sixth birthday you're grazing

in a bed of lettuce when... yikes... are those boot steps?
Is that gunfire? At blinding speed, you chase the narrative

thread down a rabbit hole while above ground a farmer rages.
Stay where you are, little Glub-Glub. Nibble on that leaf.

I've read this story. The farmer has the patience of a saint.
But he is no saint. His rifle's loaded. He waits for days.

ANOTHER MAN OF GOD RUNNING FROM THE LAW

And Lot's wife, of course, was told not to look back…
But she did look back, and I love her for that…
                                        –Kurt Vonnegut

So many have written about Lot's wife,
the man of God says, her story doesn't bear repeating,
and then he goes on to describe the pool
in which she bathed each evening, the play of light on water.
The angels who arrived at the city gates possessed that kind of light,
the man of God says, light that plays on water.

We know about the angels who entered Lot's house
as the sun sank behind the bald hills,
but his wife—
                look… how she peers
through a gap in the courtyard wall as the angels
walk like ordinary men into the house.

Such earthly beauty.
Such heavenly presences.

What to do but pull the pins from her hair,
let it fall like a cloak around her nakedness.

Lot's wife wasn't married to God, the man of God reminds us;
she was married to Lot, a man righteous in God's eyes.
Righteous? we say, please explain righteous,
for isn't it true that Lot stepped outside his house
and offered his virgin daughters to the sex-crazed mob?

The man of God sighs. He's tired of talking.
His wife and small daughter are asleep in the next room.
For weeks they've been travelling in a beat-up truck,
stopping at gas stations and roadside cafes.

Where will you go next, we ask, will you go to the little city of Zo'ar?

The man of God dismisses us with a wave of his hand.
We understand his exhaustion. When you're running from the law,
your thoughts rain sulphur and fire. He bows his head
and recites a litany: gambling, drugs, thieving, drunkenness…

And salt, he says, wearily. I am always thinking of salt.

SPUN SHRUNK BROKEN

Behind every word a whole world is hidden
that must be imagined.
                    –Heinrich Boll

Behind the word is the world, hidden as a marriage
is hidden, theirs only two months old. And behind

the marriage is the word husband—a man kneeling
in a shoe closet at the end of a hallway, scrambling

in the dark, searching for a stray work boot. A closet
cannot contain the world and a stray boot cannot imagine

light. There is work and there is boot, there is a man
unearthing his favourite Icelandic sweater shrunk to

a size that would fit a ten-inch doll. In that moment
he understands his new wife is not perfect. He under-

stands wife is just a word behind another word, someone
he once imagined. Not that he holds any notion of wife

or what makes one perfect. He just wants eight hours of
undisturbed sleep. He wants the insomniac in his suddenly

disrupted life to cease her night wanderings. She throws
everything she picks off the floor down the laundry chute.

Can't she read labels? *All natural fibres, wash by hand in cold*
water. Her thinking: there's nothing a spin cycle can't fix.

When she pulled the sweater out of the machine her husband
was on the work site, wearing steel-toed boots. Oh-oh, she

said, then stuffed it at the back of the shoe closet where
she hoped he'd never find it. It's only a sweater, she says

to her husband, holding it up to the light. Is this marriage
broken? Will it last long enough to produce children? No,

he says to his wife, sweater is much more than a word. It's
the imperfect world greatly reduced and wildly misshapen.

SHORT TAKES ON THE APOCALYPSE

For many people, myself included, the end of the
world is happening all the time!
                                    –Douglas Coupland

We stage a dress rehearsal that ends at eight p.m.
The lights dim, then go out.
The city disappears into darkness.

★

Nightly blackouts, ghostly trams.
Weary millions riding the subway
back and forth across the city.

★

A dress rehearsal is performed on the world's stage.
No one is watching. When the play's over
we go home to our dim hopes and prodigious hunger.

★

Poor actors dressed in bark cloth.
City of millions, city of endings.
It is eight o'clock.

★

On empty stomachs we forget our lines.
The end of the world
is a dim rehearsal on an unlit stage.

★

We are prodigious.
We are hopeful.
We lie down in the dark.

WHAT IT WAS LIKE LIVING IN A SPAGHETTI WESTERN

I can't see America any other way than with a European's eyes. It
fascinates me and terrifies me at the same time.
–Sergio Leone, director of "Once Upon a Time in the West"

The meatballs were undercooked. The soap stung our skin.
Threat of boot-thud on boardwalk. Saloon doors creaked.

No way out except by bandit highway. That way to ambush.
That way to murder. All the best scenes were blatantly lyric.

The dog-eat-dog plots trickled like piss in desert dust. Washed-
out colours but don't turn your back. Slaughter in the streets,

bodies raining from rooftops. Beauty so intense it felt like
a kind of pain. An absence of apples. Spurs and more spurs.

No church choirs, no holiday souvenirs. Nostrils flared
in microscopic close-ups. If it breathed it stuttered: razor-

wielding barbers and telegraph wires. Jaws clenched and un-
clenched. The landscape flared, barbers choked. Stock props,

empty cisterns. Every desperado sick with gold-lust. Children
but only to die in cold blood. Mothers but only to weep for

their children. Love was an accident that happened off-screen.
Emotions were operatic. Farmhouses burned. How to tell

a good man? He wore a stylish white coat and didn't bull-
whip his horse. Dusk-eyed Mexicans with Italian accents.

Bad men wore black and bull-whipped their horses. The stink
of machismo sucked blue right out of the sky. Sometimes

a tough-minded whore fucked a good-looking psychopath.
The extras cheated at cards or dove for cover. The scores surged

like sand, they howled like wind. Let me explain life in god-
forsaken nowhere, every man worth his salt ejaculating bullets.

Sit beside me in the dark and watch the storyline digress.
Panoramas so breathtaking they could only be understood

through foreign eyes. All you need to know: laconic men and
broken women. Overcooked meatballs. Soap stinging the skin.

ADOLESCENCE

Make no mistake, adolescence is a war.
                    –Harlan Cohen

We were girls, truly, and wore nothing but combat
boots and soft denim britches. You might say
we were bitches in lace or say we yanked stitches.
That we slogged through the burbs and smoked
in the trenches. You might say we ate roots

or say we walked ridges. That we painted our lips
and so the sea parted. Who leapfrogged backyards?
Who toked under bridges? When we entered a room
our old mothers shuddered. They fainted, they flipped,
their good sense departed. Queer frauds, they said,

you'll end up as spinsters. Exit a womb... enter a gutter.
Our shrink charmed the narcs. Our tats bled blue ink.
We were ruthless. We were fake. Dimpled clodhoppers.
And what did we hunt? And why did it matter?
Were we toothless? Were we baked? Were we hot

hitters? Our instincts were dark, our hair flaming pink.
It was spring that spring and then it was summer.
We babbled like brooks and churned like raw butter.
Wind, rain and thorns; our hackles raised thunder.
And, yes, love stunned us; it dazed us in ditches.

Rabble like crooks? Burn like braw wenches?
You might say we were young or say we were bitches.
That we dressed for love's wonder and pawed its skewed riches.
You might say we were bored or say we hewed snitches.
We wore nothing in combat. Truly, we were just girls...

AT THE GATES OF DEATH

Outside of a dog, a book is man's best friend.
Inside of a dog it's too dark to read.

–Groucho Marx

When the Angel of Books stops us
we see her for what she is—a classic bad girl
who'll come to a dubious end.

Why'd you throw out those paperbacks, she says,
those National Geographics, Art Linkletter Encyclopedias,
Adventures for Boys and Girls, sex manuals, coffee table books,
Beatrix Potter, Rabbie Burns, manuals for idiots, biographies,
the family Bible. How could you? How?

Books, we say, what books?

But we know she was watching the day we padded through the house,
tossing out books we loved and books we'd never read,
books written by the insane and books faithful as pets.
Maudlin books with suede covers and books flimsy as kites.
Some falling away from their spines, a few held together with elastic bands.

Those books fed you hot rum and honey, she says.
They took you out sailing, baptized you with hymns, stretched you
like a note until you snapped. Did they really deserve
the ignominy of the shredder?

We try to explain—
we were old, running out of space, time, eyesight...
but she isn't listening. Go, she says, waving us through, just go.

Even now, in the hour of our unbeing, we see ourselves
as we were then, pulling books off shelves, flipping through pages,
examining the marginalia and inscriptions (To my wife with all my love),

the boxes filling up, stacking them higher and higher
until cardboard towers crowded the rooms and the walls closed in
and the world grew dark...

MARGINALIA

> *A black cat crossing your path signifies that*
> *the animal is going somewhere.*
>
> > –Groucho Marx

Centuries ago in a Dubrovnik monastery
a cat dipped its forepaws in a pot of iron-gall ink,
then walked (with a pacing gait) across paper
made of diluted cotton.

Did it have white boots and white belly markings, a white moustache?

(In 15th century Croatia there must have been a word
for small, furry, digitigrade but I don't know what it is.)

And when the cat pounced,
when it trilled an almost human joy,
when its stained paws landed—

> > > splat!—

on pristine linen fibre
a scribe screamed (or might have)—

> > > Scat!

Some medieval manuscripts are marred
by doodles, fungi, worm holes, splotches, watermarks,
drops of spilled wine

> > but footprints…

No other cat has stepped so curiously
across the path of history in quite the same way
as that ancient Mediterranean cat

> > going somewhere.

ONE MORE REASON FOR DIVORCE

[Some people think] that storytelling is telling jokes.
So they have to be discouraged!

–Doris Lessing

When the dinner guest tells a joke the women around the table laugh and throw back their heads, exposing their throats. He loves their throats. The sight of women's throats focuses his mind and he remembers his ex-wife, the night she laughed at the end of another man's joke. I'd never heard such laughter, he says. A languorous sprawl of notes. Magnetic. Questing. It dazzled with longing. He puts down his wine glass and shakes his head. His wife's laughter threatened and seduced all who heard it. Shocking in its power. It conjured up visions of our blue planet as seen from outer space. Her laughter seemed to float above a forest glade before dropping to earth where it whirled like smoke skeins around the guests' ankles. He removes his glasses and wipes his eyes. Sex, he says, now that would have been one thing. But her laughter. I could not bear it.

THE BOY WHO CRIED WOLF

Lying is man's only privilege over all other organisms.
                    –Fyodor Dostoyevsky

When we walk into the lobby of the beachside hotel
we ask the boy who cried wolf if the night is long,
will we see Venus, and what's making that bleating sound?
Later, he's singing songs he might have sung
up in the hills before the false alarms and angry villagers,
before the wolf lacerated his flock. Next morning
we're riding quad bikes out on the dunes, sand blasting
our skin, when the boy who cried wolf looks out a window
and sees waves washing over our books. The room keys
are attached to worn fobs and the word liar keeps coming up
in awkward conversation. The boy who cried wolf takes our key
in his shaking hand and drops it inside a little wooden cubicle, then
reminds us he was a shepherd by birth. His father was a shepherd,
his grandfather, great-grandfather, and so on, down through
the generations, but he was the first to choose mischief
over boredom, death over life, he was the first to cry wolf
three times, but the fourth... well... we know the rest...
If there's a moral to this story it's that we all grow out of
our fables and develop tremors. Take the boy who cried wolf—
he's the proprietor of this once grand hotel built on stilts.
She's sinking, he says. The old girl's sinking into the mud.

WHATEVER HAPPENED TO BABY JANE?

Since grief only aggravates your loss,
grieve not for what is past.
                    —Walker Percy

Six months after my mother's death my shoulder freezes.
Show me, the doctor says. Raise your arm, like so.

I can't. My left side's seized like an engine starved of oil.
He's seen this before. Reads from the tome on his desk—
    Capsulitis, a thickening and contracture
    of the capsule surrounding the joint.

At the south side of the house my mother pruned roses,
her silence an offshore wind working into a storm.
Something I'd done or not done?

Getting dressed is difficult, I tell the doctor.
The pain catches me unaware.
Sometimes I hear a cry not my own.

I longed to be a spoiled child.
But. With so many sisters. I crouched in the grass
and the world came up close. My mother called
but I would not answer.

A good man with troubles of his own, the doctor continues—
    Affects two percent of the population.
    No identifiable cause. No known cure.

Cortisone? he says. An anti-inflammatory?

Near the end she opened a cupboard door—
a bag raisins dropped like a clod of earth into her hands.

Back home I turn the TV to mute and consider
my options: push past the pain or wait for the thaw?
On the classic movie channel Joan Crawford
and Betty Davis live on in silence,
those beautiful bitches with hearts of stone.

COACHELLA FESTIVAL (A SEMI-FOUND POEM)

We... asked people... what they thought of a bunch
of bands whose names we made up.
                                                    –Jimmy Kimmel

Jimmy's crew finds no shortage of fans for *The Obesity Epidemic*.
It's rated awesome. A girl wearing a tiara likes their style, says
their whole genre is great. They're kind of, like, very innovative,

plus they're new. She rates *The Obesity Epidemic* awesome
and *Get the Fuck Out of My Pool* rings a bell with her friend.
They're kind of, like, very innovative, she says, plus they're new.

The guy draped like wet cement around her shoulders adds,
I don't know their music, but *Get the Fuck Out of My Pool*
does ring a bell. Friends say, Whatever. Don't miss them.

The guy draped like wet cement around the girl's shoulders
doesn't know their music but he's heard you shouldn't miss them.
Friends say, Just don't. He's not sure he's going to catch

the *Chelsea Clintons*, but, whatever, he *has* heard of them.
Apparently, they give off a good energy and come from
a mellow place. No one knows if they're going to catch

the *Chelsea Clintons*. Only a few acts give that feeling, you know,
that good energy that comes from a mellow place. Sixty bands
play at the California music festival but only a few give that

you-know feeling. I like every style, the tiara girl says,
all the genres are great. At the California music festival
sixty bands play so Jimmy's crew finds no shortage of fans.

DEAR DIARY

*At various times in my life I've bought a [diary], and written
a couple of days' worth of reflections. And then I come back
to it and I think, What an idiot.*

–Marilyn Robinson

Yesterday I went to the mall, glinting like hot steel
and they looked at me differently, they backed off.

In the suburbs, where people eat their steaks raw,
I ponder a life on the grill. Only an idiot would mistake

a cobweb for a cosmonaut, a smoke signal for
a banjo-plucking boy. Content without meaning,

meaning without hosannas. I have wound the spool
of logic down to nothing. I have come to expect

a stupid kind of love. Silver sticks embroider the air.
If you're thinking May Day parade, woodwind and pipes,

I'm thinking those things too. And still the big question:
is the soul pretty as a butterfly? Shiny as a war medal?

I walked all night unscathed among the accidents
and badly assembled props, conjugating French verbs.

The skills to survive fall between high and low culture
and the clock on the wall means someday my name

will also be written with a slim instrument of pain:
goose feather, bamboo reed. So what *are* my symptoms?

Am I coming off? Coming down? Breaking free?
Why do I feel cold all the time? The girl in the mirror

squints back at me. Seriously? she says, seriously?
Dear Diary, when your head sinks into the chopping

block do dreams swim up through the grain
like earthworms tunnelling through dirt?

FOREST CHRONICLE

Don't sit down in the middle of the [forest].
If you're lost in the plot or blocked, retrace
your steps to where you went wrong.
                                        –Margaret Atwood

This is the story you tell when you've taken a wrong turn.
Relax, you're not a tourist here, a fictitious character
with weathered skin. You're a native
who's stumbled upon a familiar woodland plot.
Stratum falls upon stratum—clay, loam, mushrooms.
If you were a fiction, you'd be lost. Lightning strikes.
You're a familiar character. A weathered tourist.
Relax. Stratum falls upon stratum—
clay, loam, mushrooms. Deer bones lie in a perfect skeleton
of undisturbed sleep. Lightning strikes the dark chronicle.
The forest burns. Seedlings sprout. Fireweed blazes
through wide-open spaces. Deer bones arrange themselves.
An undisturbed skeleton sleeps. Admit it: you're lost.
A long-tailed hawk cries: predatory, screeching.
Seedlings sprout. Fireweed blazes.
And you, a native stumbling upon a woodland plot,
cry like a long-tailed hawk. Admit it: you're a predator.
Is this the story you tell when you've taken a wrong turn?

FATHER SUITE

A father is always making his baby into a little woman.
And when she is a woman he turns her back again.

–Enid Bagnold

In his shirt pocket, a package of Gitanes. I loved that package. Wanted to be the Spanish lady shaking a tambourine. In Canada my father became the model immigrant. Worked hard. Built chimneys for a living. The feather in the cap, he'd say, his accent stubborn. He laid brick, stone, concrete blocks. Climbed ladders to the sky. He was king of flues and updrafts. Threw his little girl into the air. So proud of her English. How she pronounced *spark arrestor, wall thimble, directional cowl.* I was polished and pretty. At sixteen landed a bit part in Rossini's La Cenerentola. On closing night, kissed my backstage hero inside the folds of the velvet curtain (how did my father know? what did he see?). When the applause stopped, I was shipped off to Eastern Europe to die like the grasses, rot in the earth.

*

Squatting before the hearth, my Hungarian grandmother ate meaty potatoes right out of their skins. Scrubbed the floors of her cramped apartment with a vile-smelling soap. Squirted vinegar on the windows. Wiped them down with crumpled newspaper until the glass squeaked. Sometimes I'd catch her looking at me as though she understood my fundamental flaw. Her words were foreign and disjointed and pierced with disappointment. At night she wept. The delicate sound of her sadness was hard as nails. She still longed for her son, my father. All those years later she still missed the man I now hated. And such hatred! Ferocious. Operatic. It rattled my bones.

*

I returned home to find him asleep on the front porch, big grey wolf guarding the door. An empty bottle of plum brandy tipped on its side. I shook him. Nudged his leg. He was still handsome in an aging playboy sort of way. The cab driver, watching from the street, was waiting to see me safely inside. I wanted to run back, ask him to take me away. Instead, I slid down beside my father and began to talk about my years in Budapest. How I stopped eating. Took up smoking. Grew to love my grandmother. I talked about my soul-deep passion for the backstage boy who'd painted the backdrop of Don Magnifico's rundown mansion. You almost killed me, I said, and pulled a blue and white cigarette package from my purse. My father roused. Opened an eye. Squinted. He looked at the faceless gypsy woman with a clinical and tender curiosity.

PUZZLE

The heart has its reasons which reason knows not.
—Blaise Pascal

Lately my sister's heart refuses the simple life,
      a plot of land, a few chickens, a goat.
It has become difficult and complicated and rampages
through the back streets of beach towns, tossing beer cans into ditches.

She has come to believe her heart is a seventeen-year old boy
in a souped-up truck, engine revving, wheels spitting gravel.
It shifts gears without warning, trashes the house,
then begs forgiveness.

These days my sister asks for little,
just that her heart behave like other sensible hearts—
no antics or sulking, no fibrillation.
Is one day of steady drumbeats too much to ask?

When she woke this morning her heart was already up
to its old flip-flopping tricks. Sometimes it gets stuck,
an LP skipping at the end. Other times it drives her
to the edge of the breakwater or back to bed.

And where did they go, those heart-strong days
      when we played house
beneath the cedar's swooping branches.
Swept and swept but our dirt floor never came clean.

She bends over the picnic table, snaps another blue tile into place.

Can a heart tire of being a heart?
Can a thousand interlocking pieces make up a sky?

A FEW QUESTIONS TO CONSIDER

After I write a novel or a story, I miss the characters—
I feel sort of bereaved.
                                        –Marilyn Robinson

Where do they go when they go, do they go asking, do they go
hungry, are they heart-stopping, are they hooligans, is it lonely

where they've gone, are they audacious, have they gone under-
ground, do they bulk up on carbs, are they ingenious, are they gin-

soaked, are they okay with this, do they lie down, do they get up,
are they hypersensitive, are they stress-free, do they go deeper,

do they go fiercely, have they returned to the void from whence
they came, do they bray like donkeys, sigh like deserts, have they

entered the solar system, applied for citizenship, a lower mortgage
rate, do they break a leg, a sweat, the glass on the fire alarm, do

they crawl along the ground searching for delicacies, chanterelles
and porcinis, do they understand that you miss them, have they

exhausted their good looks, lost their footing, train of thought,
are their accents alluring, do they have gills, calculate distances

between where they were then and where they are now, are they
vertebrates, does flab settle on their bones, what bones, are they

into death cults, flame wars, mosh pits, do their regrets beget more
regret, where do they really go when they go, have they veered off

the exit ramp, pared down their narratives, do they wear sackcloth,
are they bent out of shape, sleek as machines, sober as water wheels,

are they plant-eaters, are they bee-stung, do they lack gender, ego,
two hind legs, have they crossed over the border into a country

where there's nothing left to say but goodnight my love goodnight, like
homesteaders, have they packed up their wagons and gone out ahead?

HILDA DOOLITTLE IN THE 21ST CENTURY

In a strange way, I had fallen in love with my depression...
—Elizabeth Wurtzel

Hilda's one of those gothy girls—
ripped leggings, black hair dyed blacker.
She's more than a little glum.
Boys are drawn to her without knowing why.
Girls look at her, confused.
Is Hilda giving them the eye or is she giving them
the finger with her eye?

Friends text: *what's up.* Hilda stares at her thumbs.
Days pass, then weeks. The texts stop.
Has she been untexted? Detexted?
What does it mean to be a textless girl in a texty world?

Hilda won't eat animals.
Won't drink their milk, chew their fat,
wear their skins. She refuses
to put putrefied bodies into her body
now she's aware of her own eventual putrefaction.
She looks at her feet. Even her feet are sad.

Hilda is weirder than other weird girls
of similar height, weight, disposition, intelligence.
And *she is* intelligent so why does she keep losing
herself among the city's memes and tropes?

Hilda's broken out in a rash.
She's pierced numerous body parts.
She's rehearsed several interesting death scenarios.
If only she had an exercise routine, a mantra, an opening line.

Some day Hilda will build a small A-frame
on a nameless island with scraps of wood and her own
two hands. She'll dumpster-dive for boxes of over-
ripe bananas from which she'll make
a vat of banana wine.

Hilda has always been savvy beyond her years.
She has always been ironic and old as the hills.

What hills?

Hills. Just hills.

CABIN TIME

Summer afternoon—summer afternoon; to me those have always been the two most beautiful words in the English language.

–Henry James

June

Horse hoofs on gravel. Bike tires grinding past the gate. A mother quail and her chicks bashing through the underbrush. What is portentous here? What insignificant? The six-paned window opens onto a forest diorama. Wing is to sky what foot is to earth. If I plot a rough outline of my life must I stick to it? The birch tree's dripping ooze again. Chop it down. Stack the rounds under the porch. Red-breasted nuthatches natter like a houseful of girls. Is love overrated like happiness and sobriety? The endangered planet tilts. Please, yes, finish your thought.

July

On the back hill, the grass grows tall. Beneath a white tent awning I read a book about the dead and the leaves hold their breath. News flash: pain is not the best medicine. Face cream, eye drops, toothpaste, glue. What more do we need? Let's pull the rug out from under the bed. When the mind knocks, open: here is your disorderly quotient of memories. At the top of the staircase a woman sits at a child's desk, writing a story. Pull up your green socks, the fictional mother tells her fictional son. No one said we were born to survive. Laughter rippling up from the lake.

August

Grief slides from a mother's shoulders onto her daughter's. For the rest of her life she wears a lead cape: X-ray-weighted. Lightning cuts a strip down the length of a five-hundred-year-old fir tree. As though God were a cat's paw: one quick swipe. Get out the secateurs, throw down the stepladder, the blackberries are ripe. In dreams my voice flies up like a forkful of hay. Once, as a child, I heard my mother complain that the summers were getting shorter. Oh no! By the time I grow up, there'll be nothing left.

GRADE SEVEN SOCIAL STUDIES UNIT

A childhood is what anyone wants to remember of it.
–Carol Shields

The merry-go-round in the backyard
was once a bedstead my father took apart
then welded back together into a whirring
contraption I rode through a season.
On long afternoons it spun like a pinwheel
beneath blossoming trees, apple and pear.
He built it as he built everything else
in those years, out of scrap metal and bits
of plywood—swing set, picnic table, tree fort.
When I think of that merry-go-round I think
of Mesopotamia's golden sands and lunar
calendar. I think: plow, water clock, stylus.
When I was twelve I lay on my back looking up
at the turning world and imagined I was rocking
in the cradle of civilization. It must have grown
dark, I must have gone in for dinner. When I
think of that spring I think of my father
who died too young. I think of an iron bedstead
spinning between two rivers, the Tigris and
Euphrates, the fertile delta running between.

FIFTEEN

We don't like to kill our unborn; we need them to
grow up and fight our wars.

–Marilyn Manson

No one knew,

          no one

but the doctor
and my sister
and my boyfriend
and the nurse
with the extreme

           underbite

    who
when I started to cry,

          said,

Save the tears, sister, you're gonna need them down the road.

MCALPINE TARTAN

...it is as though the fabric [of our clothes] were indeed a natural
extension of the body, or even of the soul.

–Quentin Bell

My mother's cape is draped over a coat hanger
in the basement: blue satin lining, Peter Pan collar,
one fat button pressed to the throat.

Beside the washing machine, the cape hangs
like a ghost, the same tartan as the kilt I refused
to wear when I was eight. There's no such thing

as a carefree childhood, but make up your own mind
what's warp and what's weft. One summer
we travelled to Scotland to visit her unclannish

clan, estranged brother and sister, uncles and aunts,
second cousins, my father's almost-affair. Flying home,
my mother tore up the sky. After her death I claimed

the cape, but in it felt like a kid playing dress up.
Not my mother. She wore it like she meant it,
stepped into black velvet ankle boots and strode down

the walk, hair piled high. For twelve years
she's been relegated to the nether regions, laundry sinks
and jumbo boxes of detergent. I know you're wondering:

where's this going, what's the point of this cape-talk?
The point is my mother: hanging from a water pipe,
headless, limbless, hands tucked inside.

THE OLD HOUSE

I want a house that has got over all its troubles; I don't want to spend the rest of my life bringing up a young and inexperienced house.

—Jerome K. Jerome

He loves the house, every creak and groan of it, the wood panelling and tacky gold bath tiles. The draughty rooms and marble-topped washstand, the mahogany armoire that sailed around Cape Horn. Three layers of paint peel from the ceilings. He loves the long table and church pews, the crumbling fireplaces and window seat, the laundry chute and little cupboard beside the hearth where coal was once stored. The workmanship and wood itself, the knot-free beams that hold the house up. He loves the front door that won't shut without slamming. His children grew up in the house, their histories inscribed on the stair-treads, their names carved into the wainscoting. He loves the eyes of the house, the ears that have heard every word spoken in tenderness or complaint these past forty years. His wife's litany... lead pipes, knob and tube, leaking windows, impossible to heat in winter, an inferno in summer. He wants to die in the house, his ashes scattered in the garden. And you, he says to the old woman walking beside him in the rain, where will you be when my body's giving back to the comfrey and squash?

SWAN

Someone I loved once gave me a box full of darkness. It took me years to understand that this, too, was a gift.

–Mary Oliver

The boy bought the porcelain ashtray at Surplus Herby's, a sort of knick-knack hardware store. On Saturday afternoons men like his father prowled its basement, deep in army surplus, looking for deals on quality stuff left over from a war not yet old. Had the boy just tagged along that day or had his father taken him there to buy a gift for his mother? The swan cost ten cents. The boy had nine. But the cashier smiled and forgave him the cent. After all, the swan was missing a black bead on one side of its head. The difference of a cent meant everything back then, an offering to a woman whose child wanted to make his mother happy. And she was happy, unwrapping the one-eyed bird that would soon fill with lipstick-stained butts. Maybe the boy's mother thanked him with a kiss on his forehead, he doesn't remember, but by thirteen he'd taken on her rage, let loose a violence that terrified even him. All of this is true, even the part where the boy knocks the swan off the mantel many years later, then watches it ricochet around the room, trapped, crazed, half blind.

INSTRUCTIONS ON DYEING THE WHITE DRESS GREEN

[Clothes] change our view of the world and the world's view of us.
                                                    –Virginia Woolf

Ask yourself: how much do I love this dress?
Ask: Am I willing to risk its ruin? Remember the boy

whose name you once engraved into the weird morning light.
You were seventeen. The dress unconceived. Seek out

the largest pot you own, the canning pot you haven't used
since the summer your husband brought five boxes of peaches

back from the interior. This off-shoulder dress with the spaghetti
straps and empire waist was not your wedding dress.

Empty three packages of dye into a pot of boiling water.
Turn the element to low. When the crystals have dissolved,

immerse the fabric in water. Did you buy the dress from a discount
boutique when you were pregnant and an office temp?

Stir the swampy stew with a wooden spoon. After your daughter
was born, you continued to wear the dress. Nineteen eighty,

John Lennon shot dead, a New Year's Eve party, *Imagine*
playing on a turntable. See yourself dancing, a woman crying

in the corner. After the dye has set, rinse and squeeze in cold water.
Repeat until the water runs clear. Recall the erotically charged

face you once glimpsed in a washroom mirror, the shock
when you realized the face was your own. Stop. Think.

What were you wearing? Hook the dress onto a tree branch
in the back yard. Watch it stir in the breeze.

MY FATHER BELIEVED THERE WAS MONEY TO BE MADE BUYING AND SELLING HOUSES

Home life is no more natural to us than a cage is natural to a cockatoo.
—George Bernard Shaw

Where had we moved from? Where'd we move next? I don't remember but for a short while we were that rare configuration—a happy family. You're way out in the boonies now, friends said on the phone. You're living in Nowheresville. I looked out the window. They were right. Spiky ferns, umbrella trees, red soil, an unrecognizable landscape. A spotted dog trotted past and dissolved into an anteater. A man with a TV for a head delivered the mail. At night, termites with powerful jaws chomped on the foundation. Bats sipped spilled beer from the rec room floor. The fridge roared like an animal in pain. But none of it mattered because my mother was singing, *I'll take the high road and you take the low road.* My father in his workshop was building gigantic speaker boxes. Seemed they'd both forgotten their vow of undying enmity. When they passed each other in the hall they laughed now as though it were all a big joke, a house full of girls running out of shampoo, hot water, tampons. At the local rink, my sisters and I held hands and skated in circles to Tommy James and the Shondells. Back home, the house stank of vinegar. Pear chutney, my mother said, stirring the brown mash on the stove. Why pear? I said. Pears aren't even in season.

ODE TO THE TUMBLEWEED

*[Night reminds] any thoughtful watcher that it is in the deserts
and high places that religions are generated.*
                                        –Terry Pratchett

With each blast you fall head over heels in love with the wind.
Up here on the benchland you tumble with spherical grace.

Do you imitate God or is it the other way round?
Mornings I walk this strath terrace on which horses graze,

indifferent to the bluster pushing you against fence post
and telephone pole, through barn doors that slam shut

behind you. Gusts drive you roughly up gently inclined
slopes. Your globular starts and stops. Your bit parts

in westerns. The breeze kicks up dust and you're rolling
down a side street, past an abandoned saloon, sound-

track howling. You scoot across big screens and deserts.
Though dead, you're alive, each revolution scattering

ten thousand seeds. Tumbleweed, tumbleweed, all month
I've watched you roll across vast and holy spaces.

PASSIONATE LITTLE PANTOUM UTTERED IN THE DARK

We work in the dark—we do what we can—we give what we have.
Our doubt is our passion and our passion is our task.
The rest is the madness of art.

−Henry James

we work in the dark
we do what we can
we give what we have
our doubt is our passion

we do what we can
our passion's our task
our doubt is our passion
the rest is the madness of art

our passion's our task
we give what we have
art is madness the rest
is work in the dark

HANDYMAN

There are no walls at the edge of the universe.
  −Khalid Masood

My husband is building a wall. It's always dusk on the other side. There are no problems over there, no struggle to find the right word—mitre box, stud finder, plumb bob, screw gun. Seasons evaporate into ceiling joists. Chalk lines keep shifting. I don't know how long he's been building the wall but every day after work he heads down to the basement to measure and saw and bust up cement. Sometimes the wall is a curtain of rain. Other times it's a block of glacial ice, blue and impenetrable. He hacks off small chunks with the claw end of his hammer, dumps the diamond chips into a sack he hauls up the stairs. I'm almost asleep when he gets into bed, smelling of old growth forest. He lies awake, musing—how far will the wall stretch into the horizon? Around which corner will it turn next? When he finally sleeps, he dreams of the wall and the wall dreams of him as a twelve-year-old boy pushing off on a driftwood raft held together with long blades of bull kelp and six-inch nails.

VENUS OF URBINO

A successful artist is inspired by his muse, and his muse
is inspired by the payment of a commission.

–Robert Brault

You've adorned me in nothing, Titian, nothing
but earrings and bracelet, a ring on my little finger.
A myrtle plant grows in a pot by the window.
A small dog sleeps at my feet.
                    Such easy opulence:
roses and urns, pillows and tapestries.

Nipples erect, hand over my pubic hair,
                    I haven't moved in years.
Haven't scratched an ear or uttered a word
of love or regret. Goose-bumps
pimple my skin. It is always evening.

How I long for the constriction of clasps and belts.
The thought of sleeves is a kind of joy.

The maid's daughter is digging through my wooden chest.
She loves my green jacket, the ornate buttons,
puckered collar and cuffs. Silly girl, doesn't know
that I know she teeters behind me in high heels
and feather plumes playing Mistress of the Villa.

Fawning amateurs have praised you for centuries.
Art critics pronounce you judicious, expressive, bold.
Only a magician, they say, could breathe sex onto canvas.

Look at me. I'm rotting on this daybed, a fish laid out on a rock.
It's time to settle your accounts, time to pay up.
I'm tired of holding this pose, tired of staring out at you,
daring you to meet my eyes, yes, you, even you
who look away.

WRECKAGE

A baby's cry is precisely as serious as it sounds.
                                    –Jean Liedloff

When he stood up in the highchair
and fell forward, bringing the whole contraption

down on top of himself, my first thought was:
He's broken, I broke him.

All the things I'd broken in my life.
You've never heard such a yowl.

Hand twisted beneath the food tray, inhaled breath
followed by a silence that reached so far back

it shattered the fruit platter my father bought for my mother
when love was bountiful and luxuries rare.

I saw myself, five years old,
kneeling behind their bedroom door,

trying to stick pieces of crockery together with Scotch Tape.
When the baby fell forward I lunged

across the kitchen and scooped him up,
thinking: Why did they let me take this baby home,

how could they trust someone so careless, so clumsy… oh god,
now what have I done?

THE PINK SEA

All that we see or seem [to see] is but a dream within a dream.
                                                    –Edgar Allan Poe

A plain wooden chair floating on a pink sea, a child sitting upon it. This isn't a dream per se, it's a scene caught between waking and sleep. So many die in winter and this year's no exception. It seems the season of darkness will never end, and then it's spring and the child's kicking his feet in a sea that's not a sea of salt water but a sea of cherry blossoms the wind's blown from trees planted a century earlier. I understand that I will grow old and so will the child. I understand the word *love* and also *beauty* but those words are better left unsaid. In the end, there are facts and there are truths. There are also dreams caught between worlds, dreams like my dream within a dream: child, wooden chair, pink sea.

CAKE DECORATING PRIZE

*...[she] ...possesses that deep gravity and seriousness that
only small children and mountain gorillas
have ever been able to master.*

–Neil Gaiman

There's a slanted room where my daughter sits
at a little green desk, practising the letters
of her name. In years to come she will master
much more than the four. She will live in other
rooms, in other cities, but out there in the forest
she leans into the light of a mushroom-shaped lamp.
On page after page repeats angles and curves, unaware
I'm watching from a future doorway. And if I could,
what would I tell her? That even she will grow old
and endure the body's sadness, but that nothing
and no one, not even time, will alter the blue
ribbon pinned to the wall above her bowed head.

THE THING CALLED BLISS

How did it get so late so soon?
 —Dr. Seuss

I was in the garden when Virginia appeared from behind the latticed vines. My son had refused clothes again. Behind her, he was creeping alongside the fence, happy in his skin, only in skin. June, the garden blooming poppies and yellow lilies, the morning unexceptional until Virginia glanced across the street, back at her house with the periwinkle shutters, and began to speak of her husband, his third glass of rum.

When he understood the cancer had spread, he railed for three days, so furious at death he went at her, full throttle, a lifetime of rage. She sat across from him, eyes fixed on his, and took it. Took it and took it and when she couldn't take it any longer, she'd go outside and wrap her arms around a tree.

That's right. She'd hug a tree.

I know what you're thinking, old hippie or new age flake, and maybe you're right, but she was something else too, a rare animal who carried within herself the thing called bliss. Here, she said, pressing a thumb in the hollow below her breast, the bliss resides here.

I closed my eyes and when I opened them the garden was a blur. Time sped forward, years passed. From somewhere in the future I looked back and saw my son in sepia. Hey, I called, do like this. He looked up, startled, and did as I was doing, pressed his thumb into his solar plexus. My small naked son.

VANISHING

*I don't believe in an afterlife but I still fully expect
to see my brother again.*
                                    –Maurice Sendak

It doesn't matter where I go, what clothes I'm wearing,
which way my head's turned, north or south, if my mouth's
open or shut, if I'm awake or dreaming, I'm always with

you, on a bus in an eastern European town. Same overcast
sky, same up-turned cart in the middle of the road, hay
spread across pavement, a donkey and farmer, shoulders

slumped: stance of unspeakable resignation. Time's lost
or frozen, the traffic's blocked and the bus driver's cursing
in a language so luminous with rage we understand every

blue letter word. Late afternoon commute, men with wind-
lashed faces and women in bright scarves. Bored girls
flipping open cell phones or the make-up cases on their laps.

Wherever I go a dull wash is descending upon the same
mud-splattered scene. We're twenty-two, we're forty-five,
we're sixty-eight, but no matter, day will lurch into night

and then into another day, the seasons will shift, the planets
align, the spilled hay will be cleared for passage, the driver
will sit back down, his diesel engine will sputter and combust,

we'll look out the back window as farmer, donkey and cart
grow small, then smaller, the dead will chatter into
the vanishing point. The bus will continue down the road.

Too Many Guns in the House

TORNADO IN THE BIBLE BELT

Never open... with the weather.
　　　　　　　　–Elmore Leonard

Strong southerly winds tore through the upper atmosphere. Hot air clashed with cold. High-speed gusts rotated around a calm centre, and then a funnel-shaped cloud was sucking up dust and debris and a small child—my child. For twelve minutes his body spun like a blob of butter inside nature's blender. I cursed God and the complex interactions between updraft and surrounding winds, cursed the third layer of dry air and His vortex howl. How dare the Almighty sweep my boy up, then drop him like a cigarette butt far from the house. All night I searched the fields. Searched and searched until a voice rang out of the blackness—I am safe in Jesus' arms. And then silence unlike anything I'd ever known.

SALES PITCH

Never use a long word when a short one will do.
—George Orwell

Stun-gun miss its mark?
A good tip—
a .22's also useless.
You gotta think smart,
think lethal. Wanna
pack some heat?
Try a small frame glock.
This compact .38's sweet
to handle, got enough
pop to drill a hole
in some guy's head.
A girl wants to look
hot. This baby
matches a pink bra,
fits under a black dress,
goes to the beach, a road-
side bar. It's got that
touch, neat load
with a nasty recoil.
Try it. I dare you
to dare him to look
down the barrel of this
pretty little snub-nose classic.

RAVISHED

A writer lives, at best, in a state of astonishment.
          –William Sansom

Once, and this is a terrible thing, I kissed a girl who then collapsed before my eyes. Before the paramedics could arrive a girl died of a kiss, my kiss. I tried to save her, the girl whose mouth I'd just kissed. She expired. She gave up the ghost. I blew into her mouth and watched her give up the ghost. A terrible thing to watch a life slip away. Once I held a girl in my arms for twenty-seven minutes praying she would not die but when the paramedics arrived they pronounced her dead. Was she my girlfriend? they asked. No, I hardly knew the girl and yet I'd kissed her in a bedroom with deep purple walls. We'd returned to her house for her credit card, a warmer jacket. Once I ended up in the bedroom of the parents' of a girl I'd just met. She'd been laughing, light glancing off her cheek from a bedside lamp, an ugly lamp with a tasselled shade. Her mother'd bought it at an auction, the girl said, and her father hated it. I kissed her, I don't know why. Her laugh? The light? Her eyelids drooped. She slumped in my arms. Once, and I think of this often, she was an ordinary girl standing on a shore, thinking of nothing in particular. Just a kiss! Like a rogue wave, it swept her away.

HOW WAS IT FOR YOU?

> *Let Sex (the Body, the physical world) in!*
> —Erica Jong

Like stomping on shredded cabbage
inside a fifty-gallon stoneware crock.
Like leaves slipping between your toes.
Like being doused in salt, fermenting in juices.
Like running home after school, ravenous,
slurping down a bowl of the sauerkraut
your Polish grandmother made every October
if you had a grandmother, if she were Polish.
Like the cellar door falling shut, winter coming on.

HEARSE

The personages in a tale shall be alive, except in the case of corpses,
and that always the reader shall be able to tell
the corpses from the others.

–Mark Twain

While our father drove through the streets like the Prince of Death, waving to friends and strangers, we sat on benches bolted to the floor, three kids on either side of the open coffin between us. A woman lay inside, arms crossed over her chest. Who was she? A Bible character, sure, but which one—*Salome? Bathsheba? Delilah?* At a red light the youngest leaned over the coffin and began to sing, *Hey There,* and then we were all singing, four octaves deep, in six-part harmony, singing as loud as our voices would carry us, until the hearse pulled into the church parking lot and the woman bolted upright. Silence, she said, and began to pray. She prayed for a vacuum cleaner with multiple attachments, a tube of Saucy Mauve lipstick, a plane ticket back to the old country, detergent to dissolve the oil stains in our father's jeans. She prayed for his godless soul, our sins, the blue light of dawn. That's that, then, our father said, and opened the back doors. We tumbled onto the asphalt and spread out in six directions, but wherever we went, there she'd be—the woman with stars in her eyes—*Persis?* we'd say, *Zipporah? Ishtar?*

VERMEER'S WOMEN

Take your mind off publication.
–Erica Jong

I'm writing this for myself, for my own satisfaction,
because a family of women moved into our basement the year I was ten.
I'm writing because of their high foreheads and erect postures,
the oriental tapestries hanging on the walls.

I'd stand on the bottom step next to the laundry chute's maw
and watch them arrange and rearrange their beautiful things:
jewellery boxes, wine glasses, silver-gilt basins.
For hours the women stared out grimy windows
or gazed at maps of the world, features blurred, mouths open.
In the dim light of a sixty-watt bulb, they were sheen and shadow,
lead-tin yellow, crushed blue, strangely sublime.

I'm writing because Twiggy, my pet lizard, dined on live crickets,
and the women filled their bowls with overripe fruit.

When my father went down in the morning to stoke the furnace
and add more coal they were already up, dressed in linen caps.
One composing a letter at a desk, another making lace or tuning a lute.
A few, with haunted eyes, stood before easels, brushes poised.

Why were they living below us?
I didn't know. Didn't ask.
One day they were simply there
in ermine-trimmed jackets, tipping pitchers of milk.

Some nights before bed I'd go down to search
for escaped crickets and see the women in shawls,
pregnant or not, still working at their easels.
Sometimes, a man in the background, a shadowy figure
who seemed to exist outside the women's circle of light.

I'm just writing this because fruit flies swarmed
up through the air vents the autumn a girl in a gold turban
wept pearl-shaped tears for the crickets trapped behind the walls,
the last one singing seven days and nights before death
finally claimed it.

CHAGALL'S LOVERS

Have faith, not cynicism.
                                  –Erica Jong

Why up there, young lovers,
                                  helium heads
floating above the village?
Herringbone sky and forest of spires,
pointy church steeples...

How dare you fall in love when the world's falling apart.

Down here death combs the countryside.
Every minstrel's donkey's splattered in blood.

Come down right now.
Your mother's sick as a goat.
Your father's marching into a century of slaughter.
Today is no one's birthday.
That cake is proof of nothing.

Such wedding shoes! Such light!
Where's it all coming from?

Can't keep your feet on the ground.
Can't keep your hands off each other.
Can't stop blowing upside down kisses.

Why so ebullient, illogical, lobster-headed, topsy-turvied?

Fine... okay... stay up there
clucking Yiddish, barnyard babble.

Hey... I'm talking to you too blue fan.
I'm talking to you checked tablecloth.
I'm talking to you the colour red.

GAME

In writing there should always be an element of play.
—Thornton Wilder

Not a funhouse or haunted house, no, but a dollhouse, every room stuffed with copulating dolls. Soon, so many children there aren't enough beds. A thirty-minute wait to use the bathroom. The dolls are like tiny people, vain and neurotic. Their trash talk is horrible. Such volatile moods! One minute they're axing the tea set, the next they're cooing like plaster and spackle doves. And they all look the same—blue eyes, pink skin, yellow hair. They wake up drunk in the bathtub and complain about the view. They bite into Styrofoam steaks, then toss the half-eaten meat out the window. At night you can hear them sliding down the banister on their miniscule bottoms, shrieking, *Geronimo.* Their favourite game is Doctor and Nurse but they won't share the stethoscope. Open those louvred shutters and see for yourself—walls covered in posters of aging rock stars, cigarette burns on the carpet, a girl doll leaning over, listening to a boy doll's itty-bitty heart.

THE COURSE OF TRUE (ANIMAL) LOVE

Few things kill your writing more quickly than overuse of clichés.
                                                    –Andrea Di Salvo

He:

Bats in the belfry and a tongue hotter than a snake's ass in a wagon rut. Be still my heart, my wild goose mambo. When she comes round I'm antsy as a long-tailed cat in a room full of rocking chairs. First time I saw her naked as a jaybird the frog in my throat meowed like the cat's pyjamas. But fun! More fun than a barrel of monkeys ripping open a can of worms. If I'm dumb as a fox, I'm also lamb to her slaughterhouse. You don't know what's hit you till you fall so hard for a woman you'll eat any kind of crow.

She:

He's all hat and no cattle. Like my mother used to say—Can't make a silk purse from a sow's ear. That man's the barn door after the horse has bolted. I was happy as a clam till he slipped his paw into my chicken coop. I keep telling him, Look, honey, I got my ducks all in a row. When he comes round I act busier than a bear in a beehive. Strong as an ox? Ha! Spare me the crocodile tears. I need another drinking man like a moose needs a hat rack.

They:

Some days they smell a rat. Just the sight of each other makes them madder than a couple of wet hens. Other days they roll over and play possum. Why change horses in mid-stream? Even a blind squirrel finds the odd acorn. Once in a coon's age they're still goofy as larks in hog heaven, proof that love and hate are two horns on the same ram. Their kids say they'd stir up any old ant's nest, but kids don't know there's more than one way to skin a cat.

FIESTA

Style is the art of getting yourself out of the way, not putting yourself in it.
                                                              –David Hare

I want to live inside the movie's opening shot,
to get stuck in an endless black and white loop:
mariachi band, flapping banners, midsummer floats.

I want to be the baton girl tossing a silver stick,
leading a small town parade down the middle of Main Street,
girl who marries the plump boy on a white horse.

I want to dance to the end of the camera's drowsy lens,
hair piled high, skirt splashing like foam. I want to bleed
into colour as I come into focus. To get so close I pass out

of the frame. I want nothing to happen on this tequila-
soaked afternoon. No murders. No suicides. To be flawless
and breathtaking and recur like a motif long after the lights

have gone up. Tears roll down my cheeks. No one
does heartbreak like dusk in Southern California.
No one's as smeared with zither and light.

FAMILY

Use everything.
–Erica Jong

When the man comes through the door in a rush of wind his shoulder grazes the woman carrying a bowl of blackberries across the room. Measuring cup, wooden spoon, smell of burnt sugar on the cast iron stove top. He's saying something about the trees: Never seen such pinecones. Only a threatened plant would throw out such massive clusters. And mice, she's saying, no mice turds this year, you noticed that? Then laughing. Both of them laughing while I, three months old in a bassinet on the kitchen floor, babble on my back because I can see into a future where I'll use this dialogue, the blackberry jam and pinecones, the absence of mice turds. I'll use all of it, drought, divorce, the end of the world. I'll even use the Mason jars cooling on the counter, their vacuum-sealed lids popping in the night, sound the man makes when he does that clucking thing with his tongue, stiff muscle-snap against the roof of his mouth.

SEXUAL CONTORTIONIST

Every novelist should possess a hermaphroditic imagination.
                                                    –Jeffrey Eugenides

Once I was just like any other orchid, all sticky liquid and sweet scent, but the bees were unreliable. Capricious wind, lethargic birds. I never knew—would a bear brush against my anther, would a goat graze my stigma with its horns? I got to thinking. Cross-pollination? Inefficient, surely, and I hated that helpless feeling, always stuck in one place. I'd been languishing on a rotting tree trunk all my life.

It was drought season, the forest so dry my petals had shrivelled, my stem drooped. One night I dreamt extinction, but woke suddenly, and—I don't know—popped my cap. There I was—stunned, shivering, my delicate bits exposed. Next thing I knew my rod was rising, curving forward, then down past my rostellum. It felt strange, perverse even, as though I were spitting on my heritage, contradicting eons of resilience and hardy mutations, but I'd gone that far, so bent my stipe back up and around, an audacious rotation—I defied gravity—and then—ta–da!—inserted my pollinia into my own cavity.

Some say I'm a sexual contortionist. Others, an exhibitionist. They say mating with yourself takes self-absorption to a new level. Really? I thought my little dance was a sensible pulling back from the brink.

THE MOON AS *IT*

Get it down. Take chances. It may be bad, but it's the only
way you can do anything really good.
–William Faulkner

But was it cheese? Did it taste of buffalo?
Taste of goat? Not so easy. We were in
a lunar rut. The moon popped up, a sharp
surprise. Night was flecked with streak
and bubble. We smoked and drank. Sex
was likely. Death: the soul transferred.
Reflected light's no simple matter. Stuff
that happens is the stuff of dreams, but
get it down, take our chances? Was it curd?
Was it whey? We sobered up and set
to work, sliced it thin and shaved its edges.

TOO MANY GUNS IN THE HOUSE

When in doubt have a man come through a door
with a gun in his hand.
—Raymond Chandler

The man enters the room with a gun in his hand. There's no doubt in his mind. But I have a gun, his son says, I know how to aim, shoot, kill. The boy is the runt of the litter, sweet-natured with bowed legs. The man flings an illuminated book at his son's head. Read this, he says, before smoke fills your brain. The lilies in the vase beside the fridge stink of rot. The man with the gun looks at the door. Will his second and third sons also materialize, one as cougar, the other as wolf? Will they leap up and tear out his heart?

They leap up and tear out his heart, one a wolf, the other a cougar. His third son also materializes. Will his second? Look at the door. The man with the gun stinks of rot. The lilies in the vase beside the fridge have filled his brain. A smoke? he says. His son shakes his head. He's reading a book about nature's illuminations. Such bowed legs. Sweet runt of the litter, he knows how to aim, shoot, kill. I have a gun, he says. There's no doubt in my mind. I'm every room with a man in its hand entering a gun.

OLD LADY COUNTRY

Don't say the old lady screamed—bring her on and let her scream.
                                                    –Mark Twain

I have dragged old ladies out of their beds
at three in the morning and begged them to scream.
I have argued with them over the merits of guilt and pornography.
I have pleaded with them: Howl, old ladies, like great golden bears.

I have given them the once-over,
the twice-over, fruit leather to chew on.
Like evangelists they scream.
Like kids sloshed on their daddy's home brew.

The sound of an old lady's scream is wetter than a sheet
dragged through a mangle. A retro-sweet soul cry
that can cut an old lady gag down in the flower of its youth.

Six in the morning, neighbour George pounding on the door
with another bucket of wild mushrooms—Git out here
fer god's sake old lady and bring yer paper bag.

Some enter the labyrinth and can't hold their tongues.
Some carry regret on their backs like ancient shells.
Some pick the past clean as though it were a wishbone.

I have woken to their screams in mud-streaked gardens.
I have flattered them with pink hues and low lighting.
I have photographed them in foreign cities, astride bronze horses.

Even as girls, old ladies painted their faces to look like spring
onions. How do I know this? Because I am one of them.
Because I've stuffed myself into the corset
of every old lady chasing her lost shaker of salt.

Old ladies, old ladies, stand with me, elbow to elbow,
and scream operatically. Fill your boots with crab apples
and rain. Make heaven weep and liars out of everyone.

SUBLET IN THE CITY

You can take for granted that people know more or less what a street, a
shop, a beach, a sky... look like. Tell them what makes this one different.
                                                        –Neil Gaiman

The child who splashed through the dubious
water of the manmade lake didn't know
the water was dubious so squealed unsullied

joy and I splashed alongside him. On long light
evenings thousands of half-naked apartment-
dwellers swarmed the beach, gazing up at the sky.

All month the forests of Siberia burned,
spewing particulate matter across the ocean,
and oh the sunsets . . . the sunsets were stunning.

Mornings I smiled at the Korean woman
who weighed my daily measure of cherries
but she never smiled back. Men of all ages

pushed grocery carts through the back alley,
stopping at every bin to lift the lid and peer inside.
And once, looking out the sliding glass door,

I saw two cops, heading east, guns drawn.
In baggy shorts and loud vests, they might have been
heading for a surf shop, it might have been

just another day in paradise. I loved the child
with my life and for him would have laid mine down.
Ozone levels that reached eighty-four parts

per billion, water a cesspool, air a gritty haze,
and what was playing across the street
at the independent theatre but *Seeking a Friend*

for the End of the World? This too and most strange
at three in the morning, a skunk with raised
tail that so startled my heart I did what any

animal does when it crosses paths with a more
dangerous animal: I cast my eyes down.
I made myself small. I took a wide berth around it.

THE ENIGMATIC ONE

Every character should want something,
even if it is only a glass of water.
–Kurt Vonnegut

We partied hard last night but now we're stranded beneath a Ponderosa Pine, dying of thirst and waiting for someone to drive us to the nearest town. Nothing to drink, not even beer. Thirty-seven degrees, thirty-nine... Over there, one of the guys says, pointing. We trudge after him, a death walk across a dry creek bed, past junked cars and sleeping snakes. He moves like a man swaggering into a bar, looking for a fight. When we reach a slight dip in the earth he stops and sniffs the air. Here, he says, I can smell it. He crouches down, draws a circle in the dirt. We look at each other and roll our eyes, but when he punches his knife into the ground and water bubbles out, we hoot and clap his back. I wish I could say he's a healer or witch doctor, one of those dreamers who know the names of all the plants and animals in the world, but he's just a guy on our crew who builds little windmills on his down time. Who mixes his rum with paprika and green tea.

PETUNIA'S POP-UP ALPHABET BOOK

> *There are few things, apparently, more helpful to a writer*
> *than having once been a weird little kid.*
> —Katherine Paterson

Stop fidgeting, teacher says, you're not a jitterbug. Enough
about her. Open your eyes. I am Petunia, lover of fire
trucks and keyholes. Animals pop up around me—
Aardvark, **B**aboon, **C**rocodile.

A Dolphin

lands on my head. I stand in the corner,
impaled on an **E**lephant's tusk, chewing buttons
off my shirt. My heart is full of golf balls. My skin
breaks out in thumbtacks. **F**oxes swim laps around my desk.
I am not a **G**iraffe or **H**ippo,

I am

an Impala,

Impala,

a white-bellied antelope skidding across hardwood
floors, I am…

Petunia, honey, is that you,

shipwrecked on an ice floe, frolicking with the **J**ackals?
Don't put your foot in the **K**angaroo's mouth.
Don't tease the **Ll**amas. While teacher locks
heads with the **M**ongoose I un-

lock the Narwhal

puzzle. Asterisks fly. What does it mean to be an American
sedan, a rock band, a web designer, a leather boot,
a medium-sized ungulate that, when startled,

leaps

spectacularly?

I have been standing here longer than a talking cure.
I have been standing here longer than a mini-series.
I have been standing here longer than it takes
to paint a portrait of...
                    hey, over here,
                                  it's me, Petunia,
undulating in the wildly gathered light, wink-tripping
the Oyster beds, ears streamlined
                      for Puma speed.

The sun slides down my back and the sky turns Queztal.

Some blame the blue-veined rivers. Others the circadian body.
Me, I blame the Rattlesnake wallpaper,
which is not the same as being partial to the Salamander
love theory.
             How do I know this?
                I don't.
I'm just a sedge girl under siege,
             morphing into the Tigerscape,
loitering past the Umbrella Bird.

                That worn strip of carpet where grassland
meets savannah? Where Vole sips soup and Wombat
washes up in wisdom, where X-ray fish
travel outside the flow of...
                  yakitty-Yak
                     goes the Zebra
down in the basement where the black forest grows.

I COME FROM A FAMILY OF...

> *One of the greatest gifts you can get as a writer*
> *is to be born into an unhappy family.*
> –Pat Conroy

Drinkers

We know how to have a good time. After the third double on the rocks we go big, we go fabulous, we empty our nests. Happy Hour's a game we can't stop playing. Daunting to think of all the gin and vermouth we've knocked back over the years, the swallowed olive pits and saltine crackers, the cubes of orange cheese. Mother reclines on the divan in a white linen suit. Father adds a dash of Tabasco. They're squat as military bunkers, squinty as champagne glasses. We yearn for the perfect martini the way other people yearn for love or death or transformation.

Suicides

Everything we do is inspired by water. If you dive into a lake and don't come up again, they call you a one-hit wonder. And the rainy season's just another day at the beach. My sisters are lamentable girls, connoisseurs of sorrow, the reason fruit dies on the vine. After a picnic of tea and scones, we remove our shoes, fold our socks neatly inside. Our skirts froth like the surf, the surf rushes toward us. We tip our heads back and look at the sky. Knees, hips, waist, breasts, neck. We go deep, then deeper, hold our breath, and when that's no longer possible, the sea, the beautiful sea, comes whistling in.

Insomniacs

Nice pyjamas, we say, thumbs pressed against eyelids. Ah, oblivion. Is it too much to ask? There are only so many ways to prepare for sleep—warm bath, warm milk, warm hand. If only we could peel back the dark, climb inside. And the clock on the mantel is the tick-tock of death. We look down on the ancients dozing in rocking chairs. Admire their REM-encrusted wings. Someone, please, slap us with a new heavenly disorder. Like real estate agents, we have wrapped freshly baked cookies in red tissue paper. We have filled the vases. We have dimmed the lights.

ROBERT REDFORD, GROCERY STORE, MAIN STREET, USA

I always write about my own experiences, whether I've had them or not.
                                                            –Ron Carlson

In the line-up for beer Robert Redford says
deer are destroying North America. And you thought it was people.
                    But, no,
it's those four-footed ungulates with the soulful eyes.
They're devouring what's left of the natural environment,
the camas and salal. Bird habitats wiped out by tick-infested ruminants.

Last week, driving back to his ranch, he smacked into…
                    flash of flank…
and he's rolling down an embankment. Lucky for him,
his truck landed upright. Not one broken bone.

A hazard in the city too, he's telling you.
He's seen deer posing beside lawn fountains,
sleeping on front porches like family dogs.
At crosswalks, mother and fawn, waiting for the light
to turn green. They're coming down from the hills,
razing vegetable gardens—beet tops and spinach.
Yesterday he saw a woman running up a driveway
in nightgown and slippers, shooing an antlered buck,
rose petals spilling from its mouth.

Thirty years ago you rarely saw deer, but when you did
you'd lift your daughter up to the window and together
you'd watch them glide through the green mist of dawn,
                    but now there's talk
of culls and crossbows, hunters stalking downtown streets,
deer lurching past pubs, arrows dangling from their haunches.

Aren't we to blame for their swollen numbers? you say.
Feeding them apples, planting tulips and rhodos? Haven't we
destroyed their grazing grounds? Where else can they go?

Hell, woman, Robert Redford says, it's all out of whack.
D'you think I don't I know it? I'm the deep-hearted ecology guy.

He pays for his six-pack and hoists it under his arm,
but before heading out the door, he turns and winks:
Prettier than rats but a plague just the same.

A DARK AND OMINOUS TALE

*Do we have to do murder? Sure we have to do murder. There are only two
subjects—a woman's chastity, and murder. Nobody's interested
in chastity any more. Murder's all we've got to write stories about.*
                                                              –Leslie Ford

Tuesday. The king's maid discovers him face down in his porridge,
stabbed in the back. The women of the town rush in to help her
wash the royal blood from the royal body, the milk and oats from
the royal face. Together they lift the king into his four-poster bed.
A few days later the women return to find the king propped against
his pillows. He appears to be alive, more alive than when he used
to laugh and sing.

He was a good king, just and kind, and yet his killers run free.
The maid suspects foul play. Are the police in cahoots with the
murderers? Maybe they *are* the murderers. The women discuss the
crime scene: hunting knife, keychain, the business card left on a side
table. As they stand around the king's bed, speculating, he leans
forward and opens his mouth. The women wait…

They protest in front of city hall, shouting and waving signs—*Who
stabbed the royal heart then melted into the scenery?* They buy a full page
in the local newspaper. Months pass into years. The maid walks
with a cane but the king continues to give off a scent not unlike
spring lilac. The thick curls on his forehead resemble the purple
clusters hanging over the palace wall.

The women begin to hear ominous chatter. They worry that the king's killers are planning to re-murder him. That he'll decompose like an ordinary corpse. One morning, while trimming the royal fingernails, the maid's heart gives out. She collapses on top of the king with a sigh. What choice do the women of the town have but to take turns stealing into his apartment at night and lying beside his rag doll limbs and rainwater eyes. It isn't sexual, they say. It's more like surrendering to the earth. Or the sea. Or the fathomless sky.

LITERARY SOIREE

I gave up on new poetry myself thirty years ago, when most of it began to read like coded messages passing between lonely aliens on a hostile world.
–Russell Baker

You're standing in C's kitchen, drinking wine
when A tries to explain the New Poetry,
how it drives on both sides of the road,
collides with itself, glass and metal flying
into the next century. Elliptical, elusive, non-
linear, definitely complex, the New Poetry
chain smokes two packs a day but never coughs.
Purrs inscrutably on top of the baby grand.
Avoids trap doors, doesn't count the tree's rings.
Compelling, nonetheless, self-sufficient, gutsy,
beyond beautiful or profound. In its imageless
grey suit it struts across the page indifferent
to the postcard lying in the gutter—*Oh, my love, oh, oh…*
You think of the Old Poetry, that heavy

mud hut of desire, the years of collecting bits
of coloured glass, how you mosaic-ed
the beams, oven-ed the pigment, massed
the thermal, vegetabled the art. Sadness
takes hold of your bones. Muscular verbs,
A's telling you, anything that sounds crunchy.
You get the idea: no assonance, dissonance, symbol,
rhyme, no repetition, simile or metaphor.
Definitely no mothers or fathers, no afterbirths
or meltdowns, no rivers of tears. Having shed
all its devices, the New Poetry's empty
as a blackboard on Sunday afternoon,
a woman kneeling in a radiated field, begging
her turnips to thrive, goddamnit, thrive.

MOVIE ABOUT A MAN WRITING A NOVEL

If you get stuck, get away from your desk. Take a walk,
take a bath, go to sleep, make a pie...
                                        –Hilary Mantel

You watch a man sit at a desk tapping on a laptop. Boring, bone-achingly dull. You were hoping for a dark comedy, an endearing soul on a bittersweet journey. Something deadpan, perhaps, a little drama. The man continues tapping. If only the roof would fall in or the man would turn on the TV and see his first girlfriend, twenty years older, on a prime time talk show, confessing something. He stops to read his words, presses delete, then raises a glass of tea to his lips. The camera doesn't budge. Our hero (if he could be called that) reveals no emotion or ambition, suffers no conflict or deprivation. Your average moviegoer would not sit through this movie. Your average moviegoer would leave long before the man gets up and walks into the kitchen and pulls a knife from a drawer and slices peaches into a bowl. The camera zooms in on calloused hands. More suited to heavy labour, you think, than to tapping a keyboard. He measures flour, cuts in butter, pinches dough around the edge of a scalloped dish. Kneels before the oven window. For forty-five minutes you watch him watch the pie bake in real time. Back at his desk, he places a piece of steaming pie beside his laptop, then pushes the window open. You lean forward, craning to see beyond the room's walls. What's that? A glimpse of water? A woman's voice? Is she laughing? Crying? The man's eyes narrow, his upper lip twitches. Credits roll. You can't even begin to describe the look on his face.

TEN YEARS AFTER THE DIVORCE

Don't write love poems when you're in love.
Write them when you're not in love.
                                        –Richard Hugo

At eighteen we ran from the cities, Paris, Rome, Madrid,
every cathedral and statue a gloomy mystery. Lay head to head

on a bench in a Venice train station, shaking with fever,
convinced that if we opened our eyes we'd be drawn into

the depths of those fetid canals and never come up again.
Thirty years later I'm alone in the desert, stepping over

rattlesnake crossing signs, scuffing ankle-deep through
weightless flakes of gold. Two boys dart in front of me—

Get it, get it! Such maddening joy. They try but can't catch
the lizard flicking across the antelope-brushed dunes.

My eyesight is failing. My skin cracks in the winter-dry
air and the silence in prickly pear country is stark as

the landscape. Last week I left a message on your phone:
If you're passing through, let me know and I'll drive out

to meet you on Highway 3 above Spotted Lake. It was you,
remember, who first told me the lake's legend—in the midst

of battle how warriors of both tribes would stop and look
around at the blood-soaked earth. Truce, one would call,

and then another, and another, until *truce* burned like
brushfire, spread through the pock-marked terrain. Truce

as the war-weary carried their wounded down to the mineral
pools, as they bathed their broken ones in the healing waters.

THE PREGNANT WOMAN AS PASSIVE VOICE

Indiscriminate slandering of the passive voice ought to be stopped.
                                        –Jane R. Walpole

In the beginning the pregnant woman was believed
          to have been wordless.
Now she is refused admission to the matinee.
Surely a mistake has been made.
Surely she will be found guilty of nothing
more serious than swallowing a watermelon seed.

Once the pregnant woman was lifted above the horizon
in outstretched sleeves. Now songs are being sung
about her cravings—salted liquorice, vinaigrette dressing, white clay.

It has been said she was granted fins despite a plea for feathers.
It has been said she was last seen approaching the dock in a Panama hat.
At least the pregnant woman was not asked to leave
the casino before the jackpot was hit.

A pregnant woman is not unlike a shuttered house
being built by an Albanian stonemason.
A pregnant woman is not unlike a mural
being painted by a revolutionary named Frank.

Before she knew she was pregnant the pregnant woman
was scribbled like a love note on a paper napkin.
Even so, she was indifferent to what was being written.
She was content, knowing every error
was being racked up like a pool ball.

Who knew the pregnant woman was made pregnant
before she entered the mall? Who knew the secrets
of the underworld were being returned to her
as stalagmite and stalactite?

An absence of fish in the sea is duly noted by her.

Like all pregnant women she makes a distinction between:
I made love to so and so on a bed of clover   and
I was made love to by so and so on a bed of clover.

Radiance is regularly visited upon her visage.
Some day she'll be painted in sage and creosote.
Her portrait, *Woman as Vessel*, will be described as ineffable.

It has been said that a pregnant woman is a row of shiny buttons
on a sailor's jacket. It has been said that a pregnant woman
is the conjunction of an Italian madrigal and a rippling wind.

News of the pregnant woman's fecundity is said to make
owls more frisky, newts more sociable, cats more water-friendly.

And still the bills are paid in full by the pregnant woman.
Her famous zucchini soup is being constructed by her in late afternoon.

Many pregnancies have been reported by this or that person
but the pregnant woman has remained silent
on the subject of her own blooming.

Once she kicked her legs in the air and rolled over laughing.
Now forever is a word that's taken up lodging inside her body.
        Waiting is what she does in spades.
        Waiting is what she's become.

YET ANOTHER STORY ABOUT EDEN

Write simple, declarative sentences.
–Xavier Noria

The children in the orchard were orphans. They lived in a large, brick building. Ivy covered the walls. I pitied the orphans. I envied their tragedies. I walked across the street and stood on one side of the chain link fence. A few orphans came over. Leaves were already turning colour. We talked about the things kids talk about. No one mentioned the locked metal gate or the boy slouching in the background. Every now and then he'd scoop up a windfall and hurl it at the fence. Hours passed. The sun dipped behind the orphanage walls. I grew hungry. I grew thirsty. Well, I said, goodbye, and started back to dinner, parents, piano lessons. But now the boy was saying something about his mother. She lived in heaven and when he got there she was going to give him anything he wanted. I wanted an apple. I wanted the apple the boy was polishing on his checked shirt with the snap buttons. He bit down. His teeth broke the skin. My mouth watered. How had it happened—that I with my freedom was standing outside the garden, looking in?

ACKNOWLEDGEMENTS:

I am grateful to the editors of the following journals and anthologies in which some of these poems have appeared: *The Antigonish Review, Arc, Canadian Literature, The Dalhousie Review, Descant, The Fiddlehead, FreeFall, Geist, Grain, Maisonneuve Magazine, The Malahat Review, The New Quarterly, Prairie Fire, The Puritan, The Windsor Review,* the *Global Poetry Anthology* (Véhicule Press), *Best Canadian Poetry in English,* ed. A. L. Moritz (Tightrope Books), *I Found it at the Movies,* ed. Ruth Roach Pierson (Guernica Editions), and *The Heart is Improvisational,* ed. Carol Lipszyc (Guernica Editions).

"Father Suite" won *Geist's* Tobacco Lit Contest.

"The Kindness of Hutterites," "The First Vegans," and "Another Man of God Running from the Law" won *The Antigonish Review's* Great Blue Heron Poetry Contest.

"Chagall's Lovers," "Coachella Festival," and "Danza de los Viejitos" were finalists in *Arc's* Poem of the Year Award. "Chagall's Lovers" was published as an editors' choice.

A version of "The Boy Who Cried Wolf" was shortlisted for *Geist's* Postcard Contest.

"Hearse," "McAlpine Tartan," and "Spun Shrunk Broken" were honourable mentions in *The New Quarterly's* Nick Blatchford Occasional Verse Contest, and published in that journal.

"Vanishing" was shortlisted for *The Malahat Review's* Open Season Awards and placed third in *The New Quarterly's* Occasional Verse contest. It was published in that journal under the title "Anniversary Poem."

A selection of poems in "Too Many Guns in the House" was a finalist in the CBC Literary Competition.

Images in the poem "Short Takes on the Apocalypse" were drawn from an article in *The Guardian* about North Korea: theguardian.com/world/2003/feb/07/northkorea2

I would like to thank the Canada Council and the British Columbia Arts Council for financial support while writing these poems.

Many thanks also to the wonderful women in my writing groups who have looked at these poems in their various incarnations: Lucy Bashford, Dede Crane, Jen Fraser, Eve Joseph, Cynthia Woodman Kerkham, Barbara Lampard, Janice McCachen, Carol Matthews, Arleen Pare, Julie Paul, and Christine Walde.

A special thank you to Anita Lahey, crackerjack editor with heart and soul. Her ears heard things I was deaf to. Her eyes saw things I could not.

About the Author

Patricia Young is the author of eleven books of poetry. *Airstream*, her collection of short fiction, received the inaugural Metcalf-Rooke Award, was shortlisted for the Butler Prize and listed as one of the *Globe and Mail's* best books of the year. Her poetry has been widely anthologized and she has won numerous prizes for it, including the Pat Lowther Memorial Award, the Dorothy Livesay Poetry Prize, the British Columbia Book Prize, *Arc's* Poem of the Year Contest, several National Magazine Awards, the Bliss Carmen Award, and the Confederation Poet's Prize. Her poetry collections have been twice shortlisted for the Governor General's Award. She lives in Victoria, British Columbia.